MW00986973

Table of Contents

Twelve Steps
to
Inner Freedom

Humility
Revisited

Twelve Steps
to
Inner Freedom

Humility

Revisited

JOAN D. CHITTISTER

 *Benetvision*

Benetvision

355 East Ninth Street
Erie, PA 16503-1107

Phone: 814-459-5994   Fax: 814-459-8066
www.eriebenedictines.org
benetvision@eriebenedictines.org

Articles originally published in *Liguorian*
March 1994; May 1994; July 1994; September
1994; November 1994; and December 1994.

Reprinted with permission from
Liguorian
One Liguori Drive
Liguori, MO 63057

Joan D. Chittister
Copyright 2003

*Benetvision: Research and Resources for Contemporary
Spirituality* is a ministry of the Benedictine Sisters of Erie.

ISBN: 1-890890-15-4

03 04 05 06 4 3 2 1

1
A Changing World

"Win! Win! Win! Win!" we teach our children and they starve themselves or use steroids or cheat until they do it.

"We're number one!" we shout, and to prove it we spend disproportionate amounts of the national budget on instruments of death rather than on programs of human development. "Compete! Compete! Compete!" we teach. So U.S. industry takes our factories out of Ohio and puts them in Tijuana so that corporate United States can reap a larger profit. Meanwhile, laboring United States is left to look for lower-paying work, and laboring Mexico becomes the backbone of the new industrialized slavery system.

"Get ahead. Make money. Succeed," we're taught. So we work until we have nothing left in life but power, prestige, and the pressure of having to control the world rather than to connect with it in harmony and mental health.

When things clearly aren't right but nothing is

obviously wrong, what is the problem? When achievement is the disaster of our lives and domination its obsession, what is the cure for the demon that possesses our souls? When our relationships break down time after time after time, what is the emotional barrier that accounts for it? When we lack a sense of enoughness and spend our lives striving for what we do not have, where can we possibly find peace, feel serenity, take hope?

Ironically enough, the cure may not be in the twenty-first century at all. The cure may lie in a little known formula from sixth century monasticism. The cure for both personal disease and national chauvinism may lie in developing a spirituality of right relationships. Thousands of people across time have thought so. But if there is any truth in it, then the world may need it now more than at any other moment in history.

There is clearly something missing in the United States. There is something wanting throughout the Western world. There is, as a result, something missing in many lives. Everybody seems to know it; nobody seems to know exactly what it is.

Some people say it's good old-fashioned family resources that have been lost, like togetherness and frugality. Some people say it's moral discipline that we're lacking and set about demanding longer prison sentences and tougher judges. A few people

mourn the demise of patriotism, religion, and a respect for values, but for the most part, the values
they talk about–nationalism and blind obedience and
parochialism–are more historical than they are real
in a world of high-tech equipment, rampant individualism, globalism, and space travel. No, the fact is
that some things are simply lost forever, like the Pony
Express or mandatory head coverings for women in
church. Early in the last century railroads and refrig-
eration and education took their toll on what had
once been a largely local and one-dimensional world.
Now the world is changing even more.

But just because the world is different now does
not mean that it is better. With the changes have
come public confusion, psychological disorientation,
and personal turmoil. What is really valuable in life?
Where is peace?

The truth is that though we may be suffering
from what we have lost in this generation, we are
also suffering from what has increased in it as well.
In a culture of computers and cars and personal independence, we have not only bartered stability in
society but also added to it a touch of despair, a tinge
of frenzy. The planet is in orbit, the country is in
orbit, families are in orbit. This is a people who move
from place to place and fad to fad and idea to idea.
Everything is in flux. Everybody is going somewhere
for something else. Everybody is scrambling. Every

body is straining and stretching to get more of something: more things, more security, more status, more power.

We live in a high-tension, high-achievement, high-anxiety society. The question is, Why? The answer, perhaps, is not that we have gotten too developed, too sophisticated, too educated, too wealthy; the answer may simply be that we have gotten too much into ourselves, too far off center in our lives. It isn't what we have that is so much a problem. It is what we do with it and what it does to us. Perhaps the things we have acquired have become blinders on our souls, jangle in our minds, confusion in our hearts. What we have really lost is the sense of who we are and where we belong in the universe–and what that means for everything we do.

Take a Test

Every living human being in the United States has grown up taking tests: math tests, history tests, driving tests. Tests are a part of modern life. So, let's take one. The question is, How would you define the steps in the spiritual journey? To answer, number the following spiritual attitudes or actions in the order that you believe indicates a necessary, natural, or normal progression from basic garden-variety spirituality to the attainment of great virtue. Let number

1 indicate what you believe is the first step in the spiritual life and number 12 what you assume is the final step in the process of spiritual achievement. Ready? Good. Let's begin.

To achieve a high degree of holiness, I believe that a person must:

(a) Have a spiritual director
(b) Live simply
(c) Recognize the presence of God
(d) Listen to other people
(e) Speak kindly to others
(f) Accept the will of God
(g) Persevere
(h) Acknowledge his/her faults
(i) Accept others the way they are
(j) Be centered and serene
(k) Be honest about self
(l) Be willing to learn from others.

Now here's the twist. The document that inspired this test was written in the year 520. It has been the impulse for a pattern of spiritual life that is over fifteen hundred years old. Simply stated, it works. The question is, Are your answers different in this day and age from what they might have been when this classic text was written?

These items represent the twelve steps of humility that form the backbone of the Rule of Benedict, a guide to one of the earliest forms of intentional

Christian community life in the Western world. Un-like the 19th century spiritualities that have so marked our development, the twelve degrees of humility do not rest on a merit theology. Benedict, in other words, does not instruct us in the fine art of "earning" God or "meriting" God or "achieving" God. Benedictine spirituality simply rests in the recognition that God is present to all of us. Now, here. Benedictine spirituality rests on the assumption that we don't jump through hoops to get to God. On the contrary, we simply become conscious that God is with us, and then we can jump through any fiery hoop on earth, confident and cradled in certainty.

Once we know that God is with us, Benedict teaches, we can accept spiritual direction that brings us to self-knowledge, puts us at peace with the world around us, enables us to become a learning part of the human community, and finally opens us up lov-ingly to everyone in our life. Then, having accepted God, ourselves, our environment, and the people around us just as they all are, Benedict says, we come to the interior peace that is the sign of a life well lived. We come to humility, to the acceptance of our very simple but very dynamic place in the world.

Benedict, in other words, would want us to list the steps of spiritual development in the following order:

(1) Recognize the presence of God
(2) Accept the will of God
(3) Accept spiritual direction
(4) Persevere
(5) Acknowledge faults
(6) Live simply
(7) Be honest about yourself
(8) Be willing to learn from others
(9) Listen to people
(10) Speak kindly to others
(11) Accept others the way they are
(12) Be centered and serene.

Then, he promises, having done these things, "You will reach the love of God that casts out fear." Then you will be at peace with the world. Then you will have nothing at all to worry about. You will know yourself so well that you will be open to others. You will be totally untouched by anything that anyone says about you because you will be so transparent that there will be nothing left to lie about, either to yourself or to others.

Acceptance of God, spiritual guides, self, and others is Benedict's prescription for the humble, the holy life. Unlike modern spiritual theorists, he starts with the presence of God in us and asks us to "ascend" to the point where we can accept ourselves and everything else in life because of that.

Unfortunately, our age fails the test with

alarming regularity. We have been taught that God is something to be earned in life, that God counts but people and life do not, that the spiritual life is about "spiritual" things. The fact is that holiness is made out of the stuff of the humdrum, the daily, the simple, the true. It's when, as the poster says, we learn to "bloom where we're planted" that the restlessness stops, the dissatisfaction stops, the endless clawing and scratching for the more, the different, the exciting, the perfect, stops.

The Twelve Steps

of Humility

- ❖ **Recognize the presence of God**
- ❖ **Accept the will of God**
- ❖ Accept spiritual direction
- ❖ Persevere
- ❖ Acknowledge faults
- ❖ Live simply
- ❖ Be honest about yourself
- ❖ Be willing to learn from others
- ❖ Listen to people
- ❖ Speak kindly to others
- ❖ Accept others the way they are
- ❖ Be centered and serene

Recognize
the
presence
of God

Accept
the
will
of God

2
Centering Our Lives on God

Benedict of Nursia, the founder of Western monasticism, says that pride is the basic flaw in the human system and that humility is its corrective. Benedict makes the keystone of his rule of life a chapter on humility that was written for Roman men in a culture that valued machismo, power, and independence at least as much as ours. Humility, the Rule of Benedict says, is an antidote to violence and a key to mental health.

But humility is not an American virtue.

Popular psychology, in a vital attempt to correct the distortions of low self-esteem, has concentrated on building a sense of personal value in the human psyche. If humility has something to do with being passive, meek, and self-effacing, those are not qualities that we call healthy, let alone smart. But the correction comes with its own set of problems. Because of total concentration on self, we are too often most about individualism and getting ahead.

For too long in spiritual life, we substituted an allegiance to humiliations for a commitment to humility, as if one were the other; as if humility were a deprivation of the human spirit rather than its containment; as if humiliation were not the very seed of anger and resentment and spiritual agitation. The results are both spiritually and psychologically disastrous. What is more, they have serious social consequences as well.

The twenty-first century has plenty to relearn about humility, and the Rule of Benedict may be its best model. Benedict identifies twelve degrees of humility, twelve levels of personal growth, that lead to inner peace, to the achievement of a state of mind that enables us to live a truly human life with other human beings. What is just as important, perhaps, is that the twelve degrees of humility lead to self-development and to community consciousness. They permeate all of life–quietly and unobtrusively and totally.

Everyone has something that controls his or her entire life. For some, it's ambition; for some, it's greed; for some, it's dependence; for some, it's fear; for some, it's narcissism–that exaggerated sense of self that diminishes everything around us. Benedict, on the other hand, wants us to permeate our lives with a consciousness of all reality.

There is an ancient monastic story that gets to

the core of humility, to the heart of the virtue:

One day the teacher said, "It is so much easier to travel than to stop." "Why?" the disciples demanded to know.

"Because," the teacher said, "as long as you travel to a goal, you can hold on to a dream. When you stop, you must face reality."

"But how shall we ever change if we have no goals or dreams?" the disciples asked.

"Change that is real is change that is not willed. Face reality, and unwilled change will happen."

Humility is the quality of living life to the full, of dealing with reality, of accepting it, and of being formed by it.

Benedict couches his teachings on humility in six basic principles. Seen in terms of these principles, Benedict's definition of humility and the twenty-first century's definition are clearly light years apart.

Degrees One and Two:

Facing Reality

The first of Benedict's six principles of humility is that God is not a goal to be achieved; God is a presence to be reckoned with. The first degree of humility, the Rule says, is that we "keep the fear of God always before our eyes and never forget it." The second degree follows from the first: that we "love not our own will" but realize that God's will is best for us. Let God be God, the Rule teaches; know that God's will is best for you, the Rule says.

In those first two degrees of humility, in other words, we forswear the right to be God. It is a heady moment in life. It gives our worlds the right to go on without being controlled by us. It means that we cannot assume the right to dominate our wives and husbands or shape our children in our own image and likeness or throw tantrums at work or make demands of every clerk or diminish our employees. They all have another god too, and it is not us.

Benedictine humility starts with simply acknowledging the presence and power of God in my simple but separate life. In the first place, Benedict's teaching on humility implies that the presence of God demands total response. If I really believe that God is present in my life here and now, then I have no choice but to deal with that actuality. Life will not be resolved for me until I do. God, in Benedict's vision of life, is not a spying, crouching parent waiting to catch us at sin. God is not something that I deal with at the end of life. God is in every pore of it. God is the grace, the energy, the creative moment. God becomes the very stuff of life, not a goal to be won or a prize to be merited. God is a presence now, a way of thinking now, a vision of the universe now. God is in me, so I am a precious part of the universe; but I (my race, my nation, my family, my will) am not its center.

Suddenly, to the truly humble person, the whole world begins to look different. "The world is charged with the grandeur of God," the poet Gerard Manley Hopkins says of it, and the humble person knows it is true. There is glory, then, in worlds that are made up of different colors and different cultures and different concerns. There is glory in the world around us that we are missing if all we are concentrating on is ourselves. There is glory that we are destroying and diminishing and overlooking when we see nothing but ourselves and our own wants and whims as a person, as a people, as a nation.

Humility, then, is the virtue of liberation from self that makes us available to the wisdom of others. Humility is the foundation of inner serenity.

The Rule of Benedict is an ancient spirituality that is bent on opening us up, freeing us from ourselves, and allowing us to learn to love and to be loved. It is based on acknowledging the existence of God in a real, daily way and of forgoing the need to wrench the fabric of life to our designs. Humility is the reality that brings us unplanned change conversion that is real.

Benedict's spirituality is both shocking and simple: being sinless is not enough. It is being steeped in the mind of God that is most important. It is coming to pray daily: "O God, you are my God; for You I long throughout the day."

Then "win, compete, get ahead, and succeed" no longer own our souls, sour our lives, consume our hearts, destroy our psyches, or diminish our joy. Then we begin to be free.

The Twelve Steps
of Humility

- ❖ Recognize the presence of God
- ❖ Accept the will of God
- ❖ **Accept spiritual direction**
- ❖ **Persevere**
- ❖ Acknowledge faults
- ❖ Live simply
- ❖ Be honest about yourself
- ❖ Be willing to learn from others
- ❖ Listen to people
- ❖ Speak kindly to others
- ❖ Accept others the way they are
- ❖ Be centered and serene

Accept
spiritual
direction

Persevere

3

When Power
Is Weakness

Rabbi Ibn Gabriel wrote, "Ambition is bondage." Napoleon Bonaparte (someone who ought to know) said, "There are only two powers in the world–the power of the sword and the power of the spirit. In the long run, the sword will always be conquered by the spirit." This is a sobering thought, especially when so many of us are caught between these two powers.

The newspapers are full of gruesome stories these days. "Outraged Employee Kills Manager," "Politician Indicted for Buying Political Favors," "Terrorists Attack School Bus," "Twin Towers Fall," the headlines scream. People with jobs and money–not just the poor, the illiterate, or the marginalized–find themselves in the grip of a consuming need to wrest the world to their own shape. They rage against life as it is, demanding that it assume their proportions.

Meanwhile, people sit in front of their television sets and shake their heads. "We're a violent country," they decide helplessly. And nothing changes. But nothing changes, perhaps, because the real problem is not that we are violent. The real problem may be that too few people ask why violence is such a clear strand in the warp and woof of this society.

Why is it that, in our country, nuclear intimidation, murder and mayhem, petty politics, and white-collar shows of force are routine, commonplace, taken for granted?

Benedict of Nursia says that what the world really lacks is humility–the antidote to rash power.

The very idea is anathema to the American mind. Over the centuries, less wise figures than Benedict have turned his prescription of humility into programs of personal diminishment that healthier thinking rejects. And rightly so. But there is a dark side to any unthinking dismissal of this age-old truth.

We like power, and we spend a lot of time and money getting it. We consider it an American birthright–no wimps in our world! Yet if one rendering of humility is wrong, the other reaction is no better. Creating arrogant and self-centered bullies in the name of self-reliance is just as bad as creating simpering and insecure adults in the name of religion. Both of them are recipes for disaster.

Not only do we take violence for granted but, worse than that, we take power struggles and blind ambition for granted as well. We even call them healthy. When children talk back to parents and sulk and struggle to get the upper hand, we smile and note with satisfaction how independent they've become. When young people refuse restraint, believing they have a right to do as they please, we boast about how early they are maturing these days.

These same young people, who relied on us for guidance through life, enter middle age disillusioned, depressed, and eternally unsatisfied. They strive for the unattainable and fail in their pursuits, living lives of restless ambition and limited persistence. Their marriages fail and their breakdowns begin; they retreat into addiction and anomie and apathy–and we wonder what went wrong.

It is a sad state but not merely a psychological one. It is a spiritual one. Benedict says that the first two degrees of humility are to recognize that God is with us and to know that God's will is best for us. If God is with us, then we already have everything we need. If God's will is best for us, then nothing can happen to us that will not ultimately redound to our good.

Degrees Three and Four:
Spiritual Adulthood

The third and fourth degrees of humility are to learn to take direction from others and to learn "to endure the rigors of that guidance without weakening or seeking escape."

In the first two degrees of humility, we learn our place in the universe; in the second two degrees of humility, we open ourselves to appreciate the place of others in it too. The first two degrees of humility are about awareness; the second two degrees are about coming to spiritual adulthood by accepting the wisdom, the gifts, and the power of others. We lay down the need for personal power so that we can hear and glean and gain wisdom from the power in others.

The Sufi masters recount this tale:

"May I become your disciple?" the seeker asked.

"You are only a disciple because your eyes are closed. The day you open them, you will see that there is nothing you can learn from me," the holy one answered.

"Then what is a master for?" the seeker asked.

"The purpose of a master," the holy one said, "is to bring you to the point where you know the uselessness of having one."

Benedict's third degree of humility, too, is calling us to accept direction until we can function without it. Taking direction is part of growing up. The ability to open ourselves to the direction of others gives us balanced confidence in ourselves, the power to control ourselves, and the insight to guide others.

Direction takes us through the woods the first time so that we can find our way through by ourselves. That is what mothers do with children on the first day of school and what fathers do when teenagers begin to drive. That is what psychologists do as they help us work through a crisis in life. As we go on to the next one, the notion of crisis itself will become less frightening, more manageable, to us.

Everybody needs someone to mentor them from darkness to light, from the strange to the familiar, from the difficult to the practiced. But we cannot have someone hold our hands forever. Finally, in some difficult moment, we find ourselves alone. Isolated, deprived of counsel, we become our own last recourse.

Then only the resources buried within us are the final measure of our ability to function well under pressures of all kinds–moral, social, and spiritual. We come to the point of spiritual adulthood. We develop the power that counts, the power to control ourselves.

But we have to give up power to get it.

Adulthood is the ability to finally negotiate life on our own, to consider our decisions and weigh their consequences, to function for others and for ourselves, to revere the gifts of others and our own. To come to the end of life locked inside our own puny boundaries is to have made a very small contribution to a very small world. Any time someone fails to grow up spiritually, the whole world is a sorrier place.

Growing up depends on learning from others. And learning from others depends on humility, on being willing to submit this false sense of unlimited power to the experience and vision and penetrating heart of another.

Spiritual adulthood is as real as biological development or physical ability. But spiritual immaturity is too often ignored and too commonly confused with spiritual practice or spiritual goodness. What's worse, spiritual immaturity is overlooked in the diagnosis of professional failure, social disruption, and psychological breakdown.

Benedict is warning us against spiritual immaturity because it leads to temper tantrums and despair. It corrodes the self and diminishes those very others who are so important in our own development. It creates fury and destruction and personal diminishment; it resists the guidance, counsel, and wisdom of others. And sometimes it does so violently.

The third degree of humility can save us from our headstrong selves by urging us to accept direction.

The fourth degree of humility can save us from our pampered selves by urging us to face the difficulties inherent in that direction.

Taking direction from another opens us to the wisdom of the world around us. It frees us to go on learning in life. To think that it is our responsibility to have all the answers is a terrible burden. It is an even worse burden to believe that we have those answers.

People often labor under the illusion that not knowing something is a sign of failure. In so doing, they suppress the gifts of those in their care by their unhappy dash to prove their competence and authority. They set themselves up to fail as well. Those who believe they have nothing left to learn from anybody and dare anyone to try to teach them are describing the size of their own souls–small. Everybody has something to learn from somebody–and learning is never easy.

In the process of spiritual adulthood, we come to realize that we are not the last word, the final answer, the clearest insight into anything. We have one word among many to contribute to the mosaic of life, one answer of many answers, one insight out of multiple perspectives. Humility lies in learning to listen to the words, directions, and insights of those around us. They are the voice of God calling to us here and now.

To stubbornly resist the challenges of people who have a right to lay claim on us and an obligation to help us–spouses, employers, teachers, supervisors, directors–to doubt their love and ridicule their efforts, is a dangerous excursion into arrogance. It may end in broken relationships or even public disasters. When we fail to respect the goodwill and wisdom of others, we run the risk of making everyone the competition, the obstacle to achievement, the enemy. We look outside ourselves to explain a failure that is inside ourselves. We substitute perpetual spiritual adolescence for spiritual adulthood.

The fourth degree of humility cautions us to hold on, to not give up, to keep trying, until we finally learn the lesson of the moment. It tells us to develop a beginner's mind.

Without humility, we cling to our own ways like snails to sea walls, inching along through life. We hide within ourselves, unconscious even of the nourishing power of the sea that is seeking to sweep us into wider worlds. The fourth step on the spiritual ladder, Benedict says, is the ability to persevere because even the difficult, even the contradictory, has something to teach us.

To bear hard things well is, for Benedict, a mark of humility, a mark of Christian maturity. It is a dour and difficult notion for the modern Christian to accept. The goal of the twenty-first century is to cure all diseases, rectify all inefficiency, topple all obstacles, end all stress. We wait for nothing, put up with little, and abide less, reacting with fury at irritations. We do not tolerate process. We want power, and we want to exercise it now.

But Benedict says persist. Persevere. Endure. It is good for the soul to temper it.

When will the violence cease and the headlines stop screaming at us about the rapaciousness in our world? Only when we learn to learn from one another. Only when we finally realize that God does not come on hoof beat of mercury through streets of gold. God is in the humanity of our lives. It takes humility to find God where we do not expect to find God: in the voice of wisdom that speaks through others, even when that wisdom is difficult, even when it is demanding, even when it is unclear.

Only then will we become fit to guide others. Only then will we be spiritual adults. Only then will the violence stop and the spirit reign. We need the power of humility to save us from the meagerness of our self-centered selves, the paltriness of our small horizons, the paucity of our limited insights.

Benedict knew fifteen hundred years ago what we may yet need to discover in a power-driven society: in the end, raw power cannot prevail. Ambition is bondage.

The Twelve Steps

of Humility

- ❖ Recognize the presence of God
- ❖ Accept the will of God
- ❖ Accept spiritual direction
- ❖ Persevere
- ❖ **Acknowledge faults**
- ❖ **Live simply**
- ❖ Be honest about yourself
- ❖ Be willing to learn from others
- ❖ Listen to people
- ❖ Speak kindly to others
- ❖ Accept others the way they are
- ❖ Be centered and serene

Acknowledge
faults

Live
simply

4
Shedding
False Images

There are two pieces of wisdom that I carry close to my heart: the first is from Mary Pickford, who said, "If you have made mistakes...there is always another chance for you.... You may have a fresh start any moment you choose, for this thing we call failure is not the falling down but the staying down."

The second insight is from First Lady Martha Washington, who said, "The greater part of our happiness or misery depends on our dispositions and not on our circumstances."

This kind of wisdom is what humility is all about. The first degree of humility is awareness of the presence of God in life; the second is acceptance of the will of God for the world. Then, in degrees three and four, Benedict calls us to admit the value of the experience of those around us, to submit to their tried insights. Consciousness of God and openness to guidance are the ground of humility.

But humility has something to do with accepting ourselves as well. That may be the hardest thing of all. It is one thing to acknowledge the presence of God and the value of others. It is another thing entirely to admit what we ourselves are not; to be at peace with having less than we want; to stop pretending, even to ourselves, that we are what we have led others to believe us to be.

With the fifth and sixth degrees of humility, Saint Benedict unmasks for us two demons: the tyranny of perfection and the hazard of engorgement. Both smother life in us, trading appearance for wisdom. Both put happiness out of reach just when we may be most tempted to think we have finally achieved it. Both fuel human unrest, making home an impossible place to be.

In an age that marks its heroes with limousines and office sizes, with publicity and promotions, with status and social standards of awesome proportion, Benedict's fifth and sixth degrees of humility give us the freedom to put it all down. Put down all the striving, this ancient wisdom tells us; put down all the masking and the pretending; put down all the grabbing and hoarding and consuming and indebtedness and social pressure. Put it all down and live.

Degrees Five and Six:
Freedom

Benedict's fifth degree of humility requires that we not conceal from our spiritual guides "any sinful thoughts entering our hearts or any wrongs committed in secret." The direction is a stark one. The fifth rung of the ladder of humility, in other words, is an unadorned and disarming one: it is self-revelation, the end of the charade. It is the pinnacle of release and relief and real righteousness. Self-revelation is exactly what saves us from the tyranny of perfection. And it is essential to human growth.

It is a terrible burden to have to be perfect, to need to be right when we fear we are not, to never be wrong when deep down we know that we are. Carrying the secret of our own needs and our guilt alone is an even worse burden. It consumes us with the fear of being found out. We develop the awful need to control others. After all, what we cannot accept in ourselves, we can never tolerate in another.

The fifth degree of humility tells us that if we want to grow, self-disclosure and interaction with others are imperative. An entire industry has grown up around the need for self-revelation. Psychologists tell us that the struggles we hide are the struggles that consume our energies and sour our psyches. Benedict's instruction, centuries before an entire body of research rose to confirm it, is that we must cease to wear our masks and stop pretending to be perfect. We must simply accept the graces of growth that can come to us from the wise and gentle hearts around us. We must admit our weaknesses and limitations.

Someone else–a friend, a wife, a husband, a parent, someone close enough to care about how we develop–guides us through the morass of uncertainties and struggles that our lives have somehow become. Someone holds us up while we go on. We put down all the false images and become who we are with someone who cares. We recognize someone else's strengths so that they can call us through our weaknesses to our best selves.

We must learn to accept the grace of wholeness that comes from the wife before whom we have never confessed our feelings of inadequacy or confusion. We must learn to accept the grace of self-awareness from the husband whom we have never told that housework and children and cooking dinner for him were not enough to fill the gaps of the mind and the loves of the heart.

We must learn to accept graces of support from the colleagues from whom we would never ask for help and with whom we compete in order to assure ourselves of our own worth. We must learn to accept the graces of failure that come from telling someone of the pain our own pain-making has caused us.

Humility makes us fearless. Once we ourselves admit what we are, what other criticism can possibly demean us or diminish us or undo us? Once we know who we are, all the delusions of grandeur and all the self-righteousness die. We come to peace with the world. Once we put down the burden of perfection, we can begin to let go and live.

Perfection is not about complete sinlessness and endless strength. Perfection is about being willing to start over again, about not staying down after falling. We have a great deal to learn from our imperfections—about essentials, about possibilities, about the gentle side of life.

The greatest tragedy of life may be denying our inadequacies, failing to hang on to someone else when we're going down. We try to save ourselves by clinging to an image of ourselves that we know in our hearts is useless and grossly deflated, holding us back from becoming our fullest selves. We destroy ourselves by failing to confess the germ of greed, ambition, anger, and lust at the very moment it is growing in our hearts. We give ourselves life by working through our problems with the wisdom figures in our lives who are stronger at that moment than ourselves.

The sixth degree of humility flows naturally

from the fifth. Once we come to admit our struggles, our failures, and our need to grow, we can shed the weight that comes with a sense of entitlement. The sixth degree of humility, this ancient way of the spiritual life teaches, is that we "be content with the lowest and most menial treatment."

It is a moment of precious possibility. It means that I can never be frustrated again, never insulted again. I will never have to be ashamed of my furniture or my car or my part of town again. Knowing who I am not, I do not need to pretend to be otherwise. I can know who I am, and I can be comfortable with that. Then, if and when those circumstances change, I will be able to change with them, without becoming straw inside, either too reviled or too revered.

Let there be no doubt about it. Humility is peace. It grasps life lightly and takes it as it comes. Humility steps lightly, not intent on having the now be more, but simply aware that the now can be better. Humility enables us to see that the present holds riches for us that we have not seen before because our eyes were focused beyond the present moment.

Linked to accepting ourselves, of course, is the ability to accept what we have. Grasping for things in life has become an American obsession, the sign of the good life. Small children are taught on daily TV to want the best bikes, the most expensive sneakers. Adults have learned that backyards without swimming pools are second-class. Young college graduates have learned to expect top pay and big cars to come with the diploma. The need to have enough has turned into the soul-rusting struggle to have everything.

It is from these things that humility saves us. What we need to make us happy in this life is more than things. Life is not about having the manufactured best; life is about having what we need for our bodies so that our souls can thrive. Life is about appreciation.

Of all the degrees of humility, the fifth degree of self-disclosure may be the most American and the sixth degree of self-control the most un-American. Why not have all the things that we can possibly have? Because we don't need them. Because they clutter the soul and tie us down to the lesser things of life.

There is no time for sacred reading when we are held hostage to cleaning a pool that no one uses. There is no time for the family while climbing the corporate ladder instead of the ladder of humility. There is no time to discover the rudimentary joys of life when we are allowed to learn young the need to outstrip the neighborhood in things. There is no time even to learn the value of money when what we use it for isn't needed at all. But this degree of humility calls us to be content with less. It frees us from the cloying burden of the unnecessary in life.

The sixth degree of humility touches to the quick. Is it wrong to buy the larger car? Is it unchristian to own the beach house? Is it unholy to build well, to buy well, to invest well? And if so, what about the huge monasteries and big churches and great art pieces that are so common a part of the Church itself? The situation is a delicate one and not to be rationalized. Amassing, hoarding, overbuilding, and overbuying while the poor get poorer is inimical to goodness.

Poverty is not a virtue. Beauty, simplicity, sufficiency, and the just distribution of goods are the virtues that humility seeds. Right use, generous care, and the open hand are what humility is all about. It is about knowing who we are in the sight of God and demanding no more place than that.

There is a thin line between good taste and gross consumption, between beauty and the beastliness of never being content with anything, of having to be number one in everything. But it is a line worth walking. The challenge is to live prophetically in a world that thinks only in terms of getting more rather than of having enough. Humility, real humility, demands that we hold only to give and that we gather only to share.

Being willing to admit who we are and learning to accept what we have are the two keystones of humility that bring us into peaceful contact with a world in turmoil. It is enough to stop hatred of others; it is more than sufficient to bring truce to the hostilities that the war for gadgets fuels within us.

Indeed, "This thing we call failure is not the falling down but the staying down." And certainly, "The greater part of our happiness or misery depends on our dispositions and not on our circumstances." Or as the ancient wisdom teaches, we must not conceal our wrongs, and we must learn to be content with the most menial of things.

Humility is the key to getting up in life and getting rich of soul. Why are we taking so long to rediscover it?

The Twelve Steps

of Humility

- ❖ Recognize the presence of God
- ❖ Accept the will of God
- ❖ Accept spiritual direction
- ❖ Persevere
- ❖ Acknowledge faults
- ❖ Live simply
- ❖ **Be honest about yourself**
- ❖ **Be willing to learn from others**
- ❖ Listen to people
- ❖ Speak kindly to others
- ❖ Accept others the way they are
- ❖ Be centered and serene

Be
honest
about
yourself

Be
willing
to learn
from
others

5

The Bond of Families, the Gift of Nations

John Buchan once wrote, "Without humility there can be no humanity." On the brink of annihilating itself, this generation writes: "Humility? Who needs it? We're Number One." While we teach people to do and to have more, the streets of every major city are running sores of more poor. As a result, our society becomes more hopeless, more listless and purposeless and angry. Children of the grasping generation travel in gangs, stealing for a living, intent on things rather than on life. Surely, something can explain it all. Certainly something can stop it all.

Some years ago the country debated the penal practices of Singapore. An amazingly large majority in the United States approved of the caning imposed by the juridical system of Singapore as punishment for a seventeen-year-old U.S. citizen accused of vandalism there. Caning can cause shock and even death. But the survey respondents said they were tired of violence. They wanted it stopped, despite the relative insignificance of the offense, despite the brutality of the method. Abhorring violence, they chose violence to eliminate it. Presumably, violence is bad when some of us do it but good when the rest of us do it—the superior ones, the righteous ones, the sinless ones. Now, we respond to al-Qaeda, Iraq and possibly North Korea the same way. And two-thirds of the U.S. population approve of that, too.

It is a strange position: Once we define ourselves as good, then we can do anything to resist what we define as bad. It makes for hypocrisy, error, and heinous responses in the name of goodness. We sinners cast the first stone; we sacrifice innocent people to the wrath of a vengeful climate; we electrocute people rather than punish them; we obliterate people in the struggle for ideals. After all, we saved Vietnam by destroying it; we stand on the verge of being willing to starve children to avoid welfare fraud; we taught soldiers how to torture civilians in El Salvador; we can destroy the globe with "defensive" weapons. And now, turning a new corner to violence, we threaten to use them first.

Goodness can itself become evil. Without humility, the odds are better than ever that it will.

A Chinese proverb teaches clearly: "If we stay on the road we are on, we shall surely get where we are going." Arrogance corrupts; evil multiplies itself;

righteousness falls a great fall. If we cultivate that kind of virtue much longer in a global world, we do so at our peril.

In the face of multiple systems, multiple cultures, multiple needs, humility is not an asceticism; humility is the price of healthy human development, of sane human relationships. Humility is the foundation of foundations. It is the gift of nations and the bond of families. It is a measure of quality and a mark of worth. Anything other than humility is as vacant of spirit as it is dangerous at heart.

The Rule of Benedict spends only three paragraphs on obedience–thought by many moderns to be the arch-virtue of the spiritual life. But Benedict has nineteen paragraphs on humility. No doubt about it: he was trying to get our attention.

Humility is a process, Benedict teaches, that we learn by degrees and cultivate in every facet of life. It is not a series of plastic social graces but a way of looking at the world. It is a life model of twelve stages designed to change hearts and temper attitudes, to insert us in the universe to learn from it rather than to destroy it by our virtue.

The first six degrees of humility, as we have seen, are simple ones. First, we must become conscious of the presence of God so that we do not make ourselves the small center of our small lives. Then we must accept as God's will in life what we cannot

change so that we can grow to full stature by growing through things. We must accept legitimate controls and limits to avoid wasting life on a series of
false starts. We must persevere through difficulties,
giving life a chance to do what it is meant to do for
us in a particular situation.

Degrees Seven and Eight:
Relating to Others

In the seventh and eighth degrees of humility,
Benedict begins to teach us that simply relating to
God is not enough, and may even be a sham. Humility is not simply an affected pose in the face of
God, a genuflection at the door, a nod to an altar, a
set of social niceties practiced from the top of the
social heap. Humility lies in the way we relate to other
people because of the way we relate to God.

The seventh degree of humility tests the other
six. We find it when we have really found God in life.
We rise to this apex when we have really accepted the
direction of wise and holy others, really unmasked
ourselves for ourselves to see, really learned to live
with a sense of proportion rather than to exhaust
ourselves hoarding the fruits of life from the lives of
others.

The seventh degree of humility is also the stumbling block of the modern world. Here contemporary society puts ancient wisdom down, avoiding the moment in the spiritual life that confounds all others, the time of total self-acceptance. The seventh degree is almost unutterable in its truth, unbearable in its implications, unacceptable in its significance. It is that we "not only admit with our tongues but are also convinced in our hearts that we are inferior to all...truly a worm, not even human."

The mind recoils. What kind of psychology is this? We would rather hear "Be the best"; "Have it all"; "Get ahead"; "Be a person." But the seventh degree is not bad psychology at all. It may be the best that human experience can offer. No one can be the eternal best or have it all or constantly get ahead. The unholy grail of total self-fulfillment is a mirage, an unattainable lie, a spiritual desert, desiccating and dour. When we have to be the best, we can never be ourselves.

In the seventh degree of humility, Benedict calls us to embrace what we have always known–that we have been fooling ourselves and trying to fool everybody else. Whatever we are, whatever we have, whatever we become, we are despite it all, only our struggling, hurting, frightened selves. At the seventh degree of humility, we learn to relax. Once we stop pretending to be what we know we are not, we are free to accept ourselves and to accept others as well.

We don't have to pretend anymore. We don't have to be righteous; we can simply be just.

Once we claim our essential smallness, we are freed from the need to lie, even to ourselves, about our frailties. More than that, we can respect, revere, and deal gently with others who have been unfortunate enough to have their own smallness come obscenely to light. The neighbor's son who drinks is no longer a scandal to us; he is a warning to us of how easy it is for anyone, even us, to succumb to the pressures of life unless we cling to its anchors. The daughter-in-law who does not clean the house is a reminder to us of all the important things that we, too, have allowed to become unimportant in life. The mean and distasteful and sly and angry people around us are bellwethers of our own emotions gone awry, of the violence locked up inside our own hearts. We come face-to-face with the fact that we, too, can do the worst. We can lose control of ourselves. In fact, we have.

In this acceptance of our own meager virtues and our own massive failures, we have the chance to understand the failures of others. We have the opportunity to become kind.

It may be difficult to believe that, in the words of the ancients, "I am the lowest and vilest of all." But it is equally difficult to argue when the statement is reversed: "The seventh degree of humility is

believing that we are the highest and the best of all."
Deep down inside where impressions do not cloud
knowledge, we know that the stage we have built for
ourselves depends much on costume and makeup,
on distance and lighting, to achieve its effect. Deep
down, we know that we are both more and less than
people ever see.

Unless we recognize ourselves as potentially
weaker, more sinful, and more confused than others,
how can we possibly understand and accept them?
Unless we know ourselves to be weak and struggling
human beings, torture, annihilation, nuclear war, slavery, and abuse become virtues. If we make ourselves
the norm of society, who else can meet our standards?
If we see ourselves more like Mary of Nazareth than
Mary Magdalene, more like John than Judas, where
is room for conversion in our lives? Where is room
for compassion for others?

The seventh degree of humility asks us to accept the idea that we have plenty of room for growth.
Thanks to the seventh degree of humility, we can
open ourselves to new possibilities within ourselves.
We stop saying, "Well, too bad, but that's just the
way I am" and begin to say, "There is more that I
can be." The seventh degree gives us a new perspective on life, opens our eyes to the good in the world,
and makes hope ageless.

Accepting our weakest selves, we are ready for

the next step. We are ready to learn from those around us. The eighth degree of humility, the Rule instructs, is to "do nothing but what is sanctioned by the Rule and the example of the elders." The eighth degree of humility frees us to inherit the world, to stop reinventing the wheel. The eighth degree of humility brings us to such respect for others that we can follow the great rather than get lost making the path as we go.

"It is better to ask the way ten times than to take the wrong road once," the Jewish proverb reads. The eighth degree tells us to stay in the stream of life, to learn from what others have learned before us, to value the truths taught by others, to seek out wisdom and enshrine it in our hearts. Humility gives us the right to ask our friends the questions to which we do not want to admit we do not know the answers—how to handle teenagers, how to seed a good lawn, how to spend less, how to pray to survive the ignominies of life. The eighth degree of humility tells us to attach ourselves to teachers so that we do not make the mistake of becoming our own blind guides.

It takes much time to learn all the secrets of life by ourselves. It is a tragedy to be a world unto ourselves, to make ourselves unfit for the relationships that could enrich us beyond our merit and despite our limitations.

Humility is the mortar of relationships, the

ground of friendship, the beginning of faith. Our communities have a great deal to teach us. All we need is respect for experience and a comforting confidence in others. That confidence leads us to do what we cannot now see as valuable. But we presume it to be holy because we see the holiness that it has produced in those who have gone before us in the family and in the Church.

Humility is what gives us the vision to look upon our world with fresh eyes. Humility enables us to respect others enough to put down our spurious images of ourselves and open our arms, as individuals and as a nation. An awareness of limitations and a consciousness of the glory and goodness of God in others can make us whole. A consciousness of the brokenness of others that comes out of the consciousness of our own unrehabilitated selves can make us tender, can make us holy.

Samuel Taylor Coleridge wrote, "The idol is the measure of the worshiper." And William B. Ullathorne wrote, "Whatever a person seeks, honors, or exalts more than God, this is the god of their idolatry."

We are small and sniveling idols for anyone to worship, least of all ourselves. Self-worship is always the beginning, the measure, the mark, of deep cruelty toward others. If we really want to stop the violence in this country, we must start admiring others more for the goodness that we see in them. We must admire ourselves less, perhaps, in view of the struggle that we know is even now at war in us. Even now it threatens to take our real measure. The day we admit that, humility comes and caning ends. Violence ends. Oppression ends. Everywhere. Because first it ended in us.

The Twelve Steps
of Humility

- ❖ Recognize the presence of God
- ❖ Accept the will of God
- ❖ Accept spiritual direction
- ❖ Persevere
- ❖ Acknowledge faults
- ❖ Live simply
- ❖ Be honest about yourself
- ❖ Be willing to learn from others
- ❖ **Listen to people**
- ❖ **Speak kindly to others**
- ❖ Accept others the way they are
- ❖ Be centered and serene

Listen
to
people

Speak
kindly
to
others

6
Quieting
the Noise Within

I t's a summer night in the inner city as I write this. Outside my window, cars are going by, boom boxes pounding. Across the street, the windows are wide open, and percussion, pretending to be music, is blaring into the neighborhood. Adults are shouting conversations to one another up and down the block. The laughing is crude and boisterous. Other shouting echoes in the background from another road and another neighborhood. It is a noisy, teeming, restless, and agitated place. The noise of the streets is clearly the mirror of the souls who inhabit them.

Quiet has become a phantom memory. Some generations among us have no memory of it at all. It has been driven out by noise pollution that is endemic, invasive, clamorous. Everywhere. Everyplace. This is not New York City. It is Small Town, USA, and it blares every hour of the day. There is Muzak in the elevators and public-address systems in the halls. People standing next to you in the hardware store are talking loudly on cellular phones, and everywhere– in offices and restaurants and kitchens and bedrooms– the ubiquitous television is spewing talk devoid of thought while people pay no attention at all and shout above it about other things. There are loudspeakers in boats now, so the lake is not safe. There are rock concerts in the countryside now, so the mountains are not safe. There are telephones in bathrooms now, so the shower is not safe. Corporate offices are bee-hives of cubicles, cheek by jowl. We don't think any-more; we listen. The problem is that we are so del-uged with sound that we are accustomed to listening only to things outside ourselves.

Silence is the lost art of this society. Every wak-ing moment is filled with noises competing with themselves for attention. Shouting has replaced rea-son; force has replaced diplomacy. Screaming has re-placed conversation as the family communication pattern of choice. And most telling of all, though no other society in history has ever communicated as much as this one, whole businesses have been built around fixing bad communication when silence may be what is really lacking in the human mix.

Silence, of course, was once a thing to be dealt with in the human condition. Silence was a given. Men went with the flocks up a lonely mountain for weeks and had to learn to be at peace with themselves. Women worked in the kitchens of the world, grinding corn and plucking chickens, deep in thought, attuned to the things around them. Children picked in the fields in long separated rows, learning young to hear birds and wind and water, weaving their fancies from the materials of the earth. Silence was a friendly part of life, not a deprivation, not a fearsome place to be. People knew that the silence in which they lived as a matter of course was anything but empty–quite the contrary.

Their silence was full of the self and all its clamor. Silence had things to teach, and silence was a stern taskmaster, full of angels to be wrestled with and demons to be mollified.

Silence stood, demanding and somber within us, waiting for attention. The substance of silence, you see, is the awakening soul, and that, all the great spiritual writers knew, is something that shallow hearts assiduously avoid. It is one thing to arm wrestle the demons outside of us. It is entirely another to brave the adversaries within. But dare them we must or die only half finished, only partially human, only somewhat grown.

There, of course, lies the link between silence and humility. When the great spiritual guide Benedict wrote his treatise on humility, he grounded it in the fabric of life. He did not write about humility to make us deferent to others in all our shame. He wrote about humility so that we could come to know ourselves in all our glory.

Humility requires, he teaches us in the first eight steps, that we let God be God in our lives, that we lay down our claims to total independence, that we take off our masks and put aside the roles we play in public, and that we be open to learning from the wisdom figures who have gone the way before us.

Degrees Nine and Ten:

Awakening the Soul

In the ninth and tenth degrees of humility, Benedict begins to talk to us about the qualities we bring to our relationships with others. The first, he says, is silence. The second is seriousness.

The desert monastics of the third century were very clear about the role of silence in the development of a mature spirituality.

"Elder, give me a word," the seeker said, begging for direction. And the holy one said, "My word to you is to go into your cell and your cell will teach you everything." The answers are within you, in other words. And so are the questions, your questions, the questions no one can ask of you but you. Everything else in the spiritual life is mere formula, mere exercise. It is the questions and answers that rage within each of us which, in the end, are all that matter. "No, no," we insist. "Everything's fine; I don't care." But underneath, in the silent spaces known only to ourselves, the anger burns. Or the jealousy twists our hearts. Or the ambition corrodes our integrity. Or the greed clouds our choices. Or the loneliness dries us up and hollows us out. Then we get to know ourselves as no one else knows us. Then we blush at what we see. Then humility sets in.

For those who cringe from silence see it like the plague, fearful of its weight, cautious of its emptiness and the shock that comes with its revelations. The heaviness and emptiness we feared give way very quickly to turmoil and internal pressure for change. Silence enables us to hear the cacophony inside ourselves. Being alone with ourselves makes for a demanding presence. We find very quickly that either we must change or we shall surely crumble under the weight of our own dissatisfaction with ourselves, under the awareness of what we could be but are not, under the impulse of what we want to be but have failed to become. Under the din is the raw material of the soul.

Silence does more than confront us with ourselves, however. Silence makes us wise. Face-to-face with ourselves, we come very quickly–if we listen to the undercurrents that are in contention within us–

to respect the struggles of others. Silence teaches us how much we have yet to learn. Or as we get older, perhaps, silence reminds us, too, that there are qualities we may never attain with confidence and which will war for our souls until the day we die. Then there is no room in us for mean judgments and narrow evaluations of others. As Pogo, that great spiritual director, says, "We have met the enemy and they are us."

Suddenly, out of silence comes the humility that tempers arrogance and makes us kind. Because we have come to know ourselves better, we can deal more gently with others. Knowing our own struggles, we reverence theirs. Knowing our own failures, we are in awe of their successes, less quick to condemn, less likely to boast, less intent on punishing, less certain of our certainties, less committed to our heady, vacuous, and untried convictions. Then silence becomes a social virtue.

When arrogance erupts anywhere, it erupts invariably in speech. Our opinions become the rule. Our ideas become the goal. Our judgments become the norm. Our word becomes the last word, the only word.

To be the last one into a conversation instead of the first is an incomprehensible assault on our egos. Benedict says over and over: listen, learn, be open to the other. That is the clay out of which humility is

shaped and fired. It is the stuff of graced relationships, the genius of personal growth. And it takes
enough silence to be able to hear.

Humility is what makes the powerful accessible
to the powerless. Humility is what allows poor nations a demand on rich ones. Humility is what enables the learned to learn from the uneducated.
Knowing ourselves at our weakest points, we come
to esteem others. It is a holy moment in life. Here,
cruel laughter ends and derision cannot enter into
our hearts. The tenth degree of humility, Benedict
says, is that "we are not given to ready laughter."

The ancients spent quite a bit of time on the
quality of laughter, something that, for us, has become a forgotten value. Today we barely make a
distinction between a smile and a sneer. We tolerate
as "humor" what is, at base, bawdry and even brutal
at times. We laugh at the obscene, the hurtful, the
mocking, the weak, and the inept. We laugh at the
afflictions, impairments, disadvantages, and impedi-
ments of others because we have not owned our own
in the silence of our hearts.

Laughter unrestrained is a mark of the twenti-
eth century. Before that, laughter was a very serious
subject. Early twentieth-century photos all show
unsmiling people. Finishing schools taught the fine
art of smiling under pressure and being sober in the
presence of trivia. Sirach's rebuke that "a fool raises

his voice in laughter..." (21:20) was taken as a basic part of the spiritual life. But there are distinctions to be made that have lost luster and meaning in a culture of sitcoms, talk shows, comedy clubs, and opening monologues. The fact is that humor and laughter are not necessarily the same thing.

Humor permits us to see life from a fresh and gracious perspective. We learn to take ourselves more lightly in the presence of good humor, which gives us the strength to bear what cannot be changed and the sight to see the human under the pompous. Laughter, on the other hand, is an expression of emotion that has commonly been denounced for centuries in debutante circles and the upper classes of society. Queens, to this day, are sedate and controlled; kings, even the few who are left, are strait-laced and somber. Gravity went with the territory called responsibility, maturity. Laughter, our forebears contended, marked the vulgar, the crude, the cheap in life. At the very least, it demonstrated a woeful lack of self control. And our forebears were not all wrong. Or to put it another way, they were half right.

In the tenth degree of humility, Benedict does not forbid humor. On the contrary, he insists that we take our humor very seriously. All the things we laugh at are not funny. Some things, in fact, are tragic and need to be confronted. Ethnic jokes are not funny, nor are sexist jokes or the handicaps of suffering people. Pornography, pomposity, shrieking and mindless noise is not funny. Derision, sneers, sarcasm, and snide remarks, no matter how witty, pointed, clever, or cutting, are not funny. Beavis and Butt-head are not funny; they are cruel. They are designed to cheapen the dearest parts of life. They are arrogant usurpers of God's right to judgment, and they do it under a false face of joy, a patina of happiness, a sheen of goodwill. They are the most dishonest of dishonesties.

The humble person, Benedict reminds us, never uses speech to grind another person to dust, never laughs the nervous laugh of scorn. The humble person cultivates a soul in which everyone is safe. A humble person handles the presence of the other with soft hands, a velvet heart, and an unveiled mind.

With silence and a smile, humble people come to grips with the acid in themselves and bring balm to those whose hearts would break from ridicule. With silence and a smile, pomposity shatters, pretentiousness fades, and I am freed to tender my woundedness to the care of the world so that the wounded of the world can find care in me.

And how does it happen? Benedict is very clear: we surrender to God, we surrender to the wisdom of others, we surrender our masks, we surrender the noise that becomes the shield between us and our deepest selves. We become whole in the acceptance of our own brokenness. The more we treat gently our own incomplete selves, the gentler we are with those around us. What we do not expect of ourselves, we will not expect of others. What we do not find in ourselves, we will not demand of others. What we know to be the fruit of great struggle, we will come to appreciate in others.

The quality of our care for others emerges in direct correlation to our acceptance of ourselves in our totality, our dark side with the bright, the rough side with the smooth, the cultivated with the unfinished in us, not because we find ourselves perfect, but precisely because we do not. Once upon a time, the ancients tell, a rabbi gave a coin to a dissolute beggar and was roundly criticized for being soft. "Shall I be more finicky than God, who gave the coin to me?" he asked.

Silence is a cornerstone of Benedictine life and social development, but the goal of Benedictine spirituality is not non-talking. The goal of monastic silence and monastic speech is respect for others, a sense of place, a spirit of peace. The rule does not call for absolute silence; it calls for thoughtful talk. Silence for its own selfish, insulating sake, silence that is passive-aggressive, silence that is insensitive to the present needs of the other is not Benedictine silence.

Benedictine spirituality forms us to listen always for the voice of God around us and in us. When my own noise is what drowns that word out, the spiritual life becomes a sham. Benedictine spirituality forms us to know our place in the world. When we refuse to give place to others, when we consume all the space of our worlds with our own sounds, our own truths, our own wisdom, and our own ideas, there is no room for anyone else's ideas. When a person debates contentiously with anyone, let alone with the teachers and the guides of this life, the ego becomes a majority of one and there is no one left from whom to learn. But Benedictine spirituality is a builder of human community. When talk is unrestrained and gossip becomes the food of the soul, then the destruction of others can't be far behind. When talk is loud and boisterous, when we make light of everything, when nothing is sacred or spared the raillery of a joke, the seriousness of all life is at stake, and our spirits wither from a lack of beauty and substance.

Make no doubt about it, the ability to listen to another, to sit silently in the presence of God, to give sober heed, and to ponder is the nucleus of Benedictine spirituality. It may, in fact, be what is most missing in a century saturated with information, sated with noise, but short on reflection. The Word we seek is speaking in the silence within us. Blocking it out and relinquishing the spirit of silence numbs the Benedictine heart in a noise-numbed world.

The ancients wrote: Once upon a time, a disciple asked the elder, "How shall I experience my oneness with creation?" and the elder answered, "By listening."

The disciple pressed the point: "But how am I to listen?"

And the elder taught, "Become an ear that pays attention to every single thing the universe is saying. The moment you hear something you yourself are saying, stop."

Humility stretches the mind to listen to the noise within us that needs quieting. Humility attunes us to the wisdom from outside ourselves that needs to be learned. Humility saves us before we drown our hearts in the noise of our own confusions.

The Twelve Steps

of Humility

- ❖ Recognize the presence of God
- ❖ Accept the will of God
- ❖ Accept spiritual direction
- ❖ Persevere
- ❖ Acknowledge faults
- ❖ Live simply
- ❖ Be honest about yourself
- ❖ Be willing to learn from others
- ❖ Listen to people
- ❖ Speak kindly to others
- ❖ **Accept others the way they are**
- ❖ **Be centered and serene**

Accept
others
the way
they are

Be
centered
and
serene

7

To Live
in God's Presence

"All cruelty springs from hard-heartedness and weakness," Seneca, the Roman orator, wrote. It is not something we like to think about. We so often call cruelty "justice" that we have forgotten how really destructive we can be. We break off relationships with our children and lovers in order to punish them; we take delight in the execution of the retarded and the poor in the name of eradicating evil from society; we destroy people's reputations with impunity in the name of truth. Worse than that, we forget how really far we ourselves are from the spiritual life and spiritual maturity and spiritual vision when we do these things.

Benedict knew the connection between cruelty and spiritual development very well. He recognized it keenly, in fact. In the chapter on the twelve degrees of humility, which crowns the seven chapters on the spiritual life in the Rule of Benedict, he does one of the most surprising things in the spiritual literature of the Church. He teaches that the first step of the spiritual life lies simply in recognizing the presence of God, yes; but he makes a more pointed statement than that. The acme, the ultimate, the high point of our spiritual development he defines as kindness of speech and serenity of soul.

It's clear, then, why Benedict's eleventh degree of humility requires that we treat all people with respect. It's obvious, then, why Benedict's twelfth degree of humility is about the attainment of serenity and calm and personal simplicity. The fact is that we cannot accept others and we cannot be serene in life until we know ourselves with ruthless but gentle honesty and accept the will of God with unlimited and unending abandon. The way we deal with others measures our real holiness. The degree to which we see the presence of God in all things gauges our real union with God. These degrees are the epitome. The attainment of these last degrees of humility is the final test of our spiritual sincerity, our spiritual mettle.

The presentation startles. After all, our generation, the age of assembly lines and mechanical processes, describes life–all life–in terms of progress from the simple to the complex, from the effortless to the difficult, from the obvious to the complicated. People are obvious, God is complicated, we assume. Human relationships are simple, the spiritual life is complex, we judge. Living with others is normal, attaining God is difficult, we teach. It seems, then, that learning to live well with the simple, the obvious, and the "real" is basic. Learning to know and experience God is the murky, the mysterious, the mystical part of our very unmystical lives.

But Benedict, the monastic mentor, teaches exactly the opposite. Because God is everywhere, God is surely here. Now; always. With me as I write; with you as you read. I don't have to perform esoteric spiritual exercises to earn God. I don't have to pass tests and do hard things, pass tests and prove myself, pass tests and become perfect. I simply have to live in the Presence. Then no test is too difficult for me. No effort is too much. No proof is required. No perfection is necessary. Living consciously in the presence of God, I begin to see through the eyes of God and live the mind of God. I become a contemplative.

Then if I allow myself to sink into God, life suddenly becomes livable. Not necessarily easier, perhaps. The monthly bills are still bills; pain is still pain; difficult relationships are still difficult. But I am changed. I am more capable now of dealing with them. I have more vision, more hope, more endurance, and more courage to change what needs to be changed

Degrees Eleven and Twelve:

Kindness and Serenity

Suddenly the eleventh degree of humility shines with another glow. We begin to see that the spiritual life is more than the development of a pious relationship with God, which is more designed to make us feel good than to make us holy. The spiritual life–both its measure and its meaning–depends on the way we relate to one another. It is in the other that the will of God resides. To ridicule another, then, is to deride the will of God. Anyone we reject is a missed message in our lives. We have seen it in the other–and refused it. We have seen another's needs and refused compassion. We have seen another's hurts and refused understanding. We have seen another's anger and refused to listen. We have seen another's gifts and refused to acknowledge them.

We have failed to revere the sanctifying place of others in our lives. Ridicule is the poison of the soul.

Others are the bridge to our own development. They make up what is wanting in us. They demand new insights in us, new awareness, new skills of patience and acceptance. They require us to overcome our revulsions, to risk a wild trust, to take down the barriers in our lives. They teach us to let differences in so that we do not all die of the breathless white space with which we surround ourselves. They enable us to take on the heart of God for them.

Most of all, other people teach us that no one has the right to take up all the space in life. There are other ideas, other ways of doing things, other needs and desires than ours in life. It is a painful moment, this time of testing the truth of what we say we believe. It comes at odd times: when we are tempted to ignore the appeals for alms because we are tired of giving to the "shiftless." It comes when we are intent on having our own way. It comes when we resist the chance to hire women and minorities. It comes when we are tempted to tell the latest ethnic joke that ridicules and reduces to dust a whole class of people.

Indeed, the reverent acceptance of the other is the last and final step to a life lived totally in God.

Finally, the sage Benedict teaches, the twelfth degree of humility marks our genuine growth, our real depth. We must learn, it instructs, to be a peaceful presence in the world so that the world can really be a more peaceful place because of us. We have to learn to stop banging doors and whistling in cemeteries. We have to quit getting hysterical every time the phone rings or the schedule changes. We have to quit strutting and complaining, agitating and fomenting trouble in the neighborhood and the office and the bridge club. Where we walk, other people must be safe. When we come into a room, every stomach should not tighten in fear for their reputation or their self-esteem or their peace of mind.

A gentle presence brings everyone to a sense of the sacred in life. When people carry themselves with a quiet and gentle presence, the whole world knows that it is safe from domination; it breathes a little easier and sleeps a little more soundly and feels a little more serenity itself. An accepting presence gives the rest of the world permission to be accepting too. Perhaps Helen Keller taught us all we need to know about humility when she wrote: "I thank God for my handicaps, for through them I have found myself, my work and my God." The acceptance of handicaps–our own and others'–is the meaning of humility.

Humility connects us to the world and makes the world connected, a good and gracious space.

Humility calms us and it calms others. It inspires and it assures; it enriches and it enables.

Humility gifts us with happiness and graces the world with peace. Best of all, its attainment is in our own hands. Who can ask for more?